Classical Jazz Rags & Blues

9 Classical Melodies Arranged in Jazz Styles for Late Intermediate Pianists

MARTHA MIER

Revisit the classical melodies found in this collection and experience them in very different and exciting settings! In *Classical Jazz, Rags & Blues, Book 5*, familiar melodies from piano literature, opera, and orchestral repertoire are arranged in jazz styles, including ragtime and blues. Students who previously have learned some of these gems will love to revisit them in new styles. Students playing these pieces for the first time will become familiar with these wonderful melodies.

It is my hope that students will enjoy playing these arrangements and gain a greater appreciation for these timeless classical themes.

Boogie for Elise (Beethoven: Für Elise, WoO 59) 20
Habanera Boogie (Bizet: Habanera) 5
Jazzy French Song (Tchaikovsky: Old French Song, Op. 39, No. 16). .14
Jazzy Sonata (Mozart: Sonata in A Major, K. 331) 11
Lively Sonatina (Attwood: Sonatina No. 3 in F Major). 16
Perky Turkish March (Beethoven: Turkish March). 22
Ragtime Penny (Beethoven: Rondo a Capriccio, Op. 129) 8
Ragtime Surprise (Haydn: Symphony No. 94, *The Surprise*). 2
Träumerei Dreams (Schumann: Träumerei, Op. 15, No. 7) 18

Alfred Music Publishing Co., Inc.
P.O. Box 10003
Van Nuys, CA 91410-0003
alfred.com

ISBN-10: 0-7390-8921-8
ISBN-13: 978-0-7390-8921-7

RAGTIME SURPRISE

(Based on the second movement of "Symphony No. 94 in G Major, *The Surprise*")

Franz Joseph Haydn
(1732–1809)
Arr. by Martha Mier

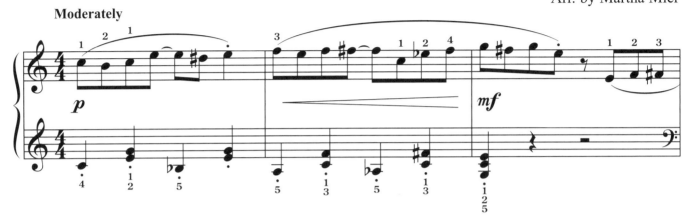

3

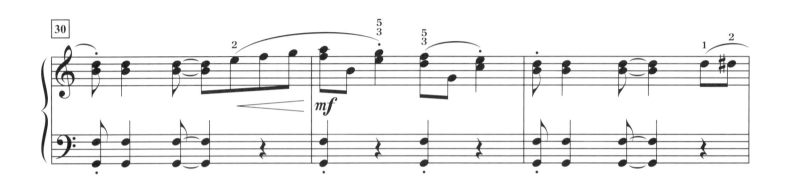

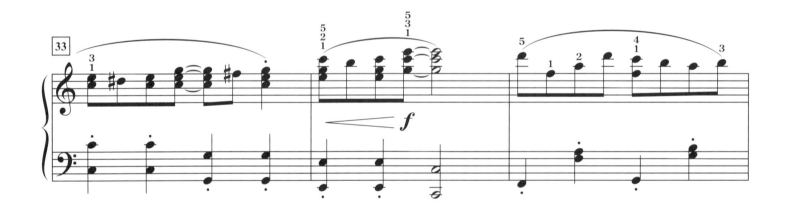

Habanera Boogie

(Based on "Habanera" from the opera *Carmen*)

George Bizet
(1838–1875)
Arr. by Martha Mier

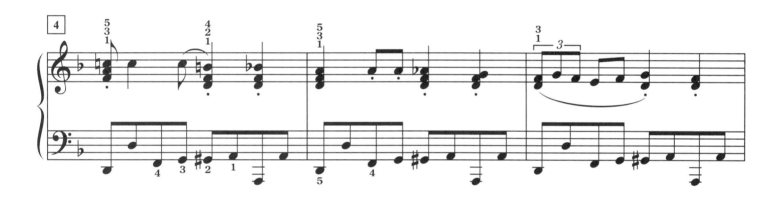

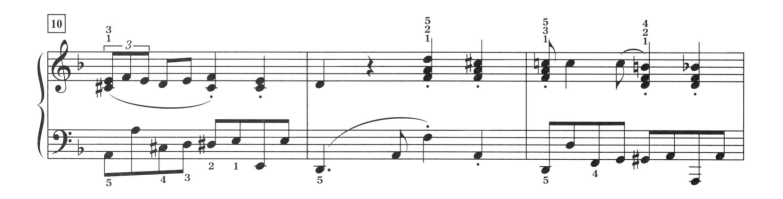

RAGTIME PENNY

(Based on the piano solo "Rondo a capriccio, Op. 129, Rage Over a Lost Penny")

Ludwig van Beethoven
(1770–1827)
Arr. by Martha Mier

Fast and agitated

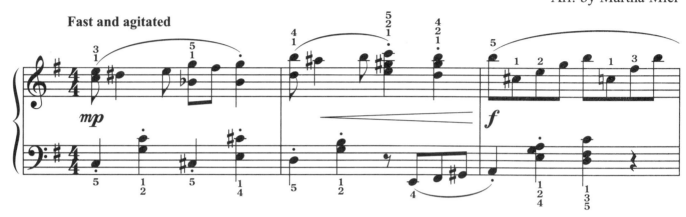

Jazzy Sonata

(Based on the first movement of "Sonata in A Major, K. 331" for piano)

Wolfgang Amadeus Mozart
(1756–1791)
Arr. by Martha Mier

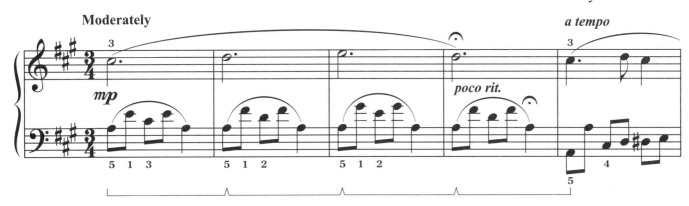

Jazzy French Song

(Based on the piano solo "Old French Song, Op. 39, No. 16," from *Album for the Young*)

Peter Ilyich Tchaikovsky
(1840–1893)
Arr. by Martha Mier

Lively Sonatina

(Based on the third movement of "Sonatina No. 3 in F Major" for piano)

Thomas Attwood
(1765–1838)
Arr. by Martha Mier

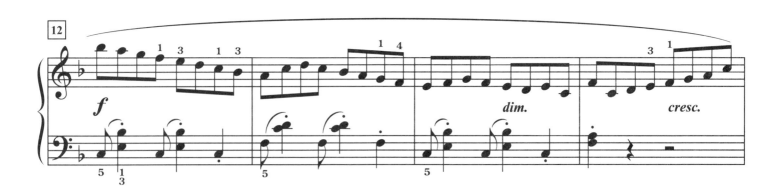

Träumerei Dreams

(Based on the piano solo "Träumerei, Op. 15, No. 7," from *Scenes from Childhood*)

Robert Schumann
(1810–1856)
Arr. by Martha Mier

Boogie for Elise

(Based on the piano solo "Für Elise, WoO 59")

Ludwig van Beethoven
(1770–1827)
Arr. by Martha Mier

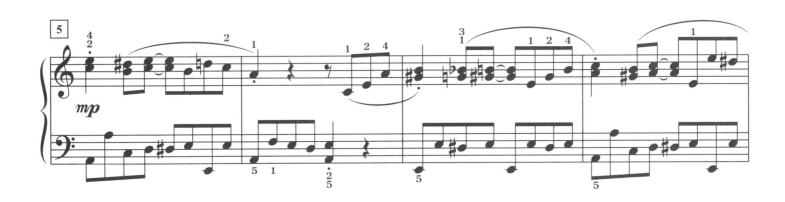

Perky Turkish March

(Based on the "Turkish March" from the orchestral music for the play *The Ruins of Athens*)

Ludwig van Beethoven
(1770–1827)
Arr. by Martha Mier

Moderately fast

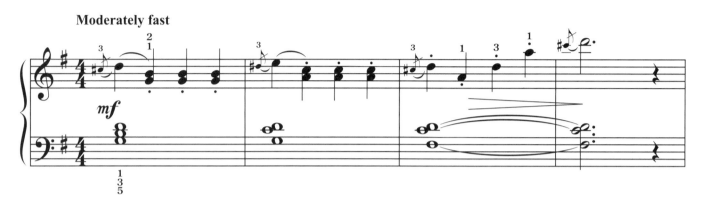

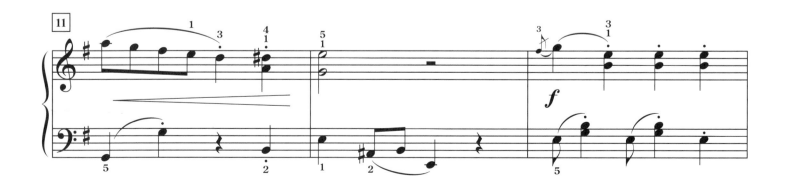